Metaverse Crypto For Beginners

Adidas Wilson

Published by Adidas Wilson, 2022.

Adidas Wilson
P.O. Box 2266
Antioch, Tn. 37011
siriusvisionstudios@gmail.com
www.adidaswilson.com

METAVERSE CRYPTO FOR BEGINNERS

First edition. January 9, 2022.

ISBN: 979-8201782061

Written by Adidas Wilson.

Table of Contents

Preface

Do We Live in the Matrix? There are tests that can be used to show whether human beings are a part of a huge computer simulation. However, the big question is: do you want to know? In the Matrix, a 1991 sci-fi film, Neo, the protagonist, is shocked to see humans defying Physics laws. They vanish suddenly and run up walls. Neo is unaware but his consciousness is encapsulated in the Matrix (some virtual reality simulation made by sentient machines). Things get interesting when Neo is offered two options: choose the red pill and learn the entire truth concerning the Matrix or choose the blue pill and go back to his initial oblivious state. Today, Physicists can give you the same choice: there is a way to test whether humans are living in a Matrix. This can be done by studying space radiation. Although this sounds like fiction, some philosophers believe there is a higher chance of humans being artificial intelligences than there is of us being organic minds. If this were the case, the programmers would be like gods to humans with the ability to twist reality whenever they want. So, which is the better option, to know the whole truth or leave things as they are? In 2001, the first serious step was taken to try and know the truth. Experts attempted to estimate the number of resources required for a universe-size simulation. This made it look impossible. Recreating the universe—from the big bang to this moment—would require more energy than is available in the universe. This is the opinion of an MIT quantum-mechanical engineer. However, other experts realized that it is possible to replicate the universe just enough to fool the inhabitants— it does not have to be a perfect copy. Besides, the computational power needed would be less. There are supercomputers in this age that replicate the universe in its initial stages. The technology is advancing rapidly. Would you believe that your cell phone's processing power is more than that of NASA's computers during the moon landing? Silas Beane believes that in a century, they may have the technology to have humans in their simulation boxes. Very soon, the only barrier to taking this step could be social mores and legislation. According to John D. Barrow, a simulation of reality would not be without glitches. The operating system of the universe would need to be updated occasionally. Together with his colleagues, they suggested what they referred to as a more concrete simulation test. It is assumed that space is smooth and infinite. It would be difficult to replicate this, and so physicists will have to make up simulated space. Is the universe a simulation? Was it birthed at the big bang? Beane believes that it does not matter what the answer (or belief is). A cosmic ray test can clear things up. A weirder question is: what if the universe's simulators are simulations as well? So, would you like to know?

Introduction

Meta: What Exactly Is the Metaverse and How Will It Affect Your Brand? For the longest time, Facebook has been leading in social interaction along with its other apps, WhatsApp, and Instagram. They have played a huge part in making the world a global village. Mark Zuckerberg and his team have discovered the potential in the metaverse and want to be a part of it. So, what is the metaverse all about? The term metaverse was first used in 1992 in a science fiction novel called snow crash. It portrayed humans as avatars where they interacted with each other and software agents which HBO network is looking to produce into a television series. In a more detailed explanation, the metaverse combines technologies that include virtual reality, which consists of an online community where users interact with each other in a simulated world of augmented reality that combines both the physical and the digital world. In other words, it is how we interact with each other through technology. Mark Zuckerberg intends on bringing it to reality. This way, we can connect and share our thoughts and imaginations through augmented reality (AR). Now that we are in the 21st century, the metaverse is believed to be our future. With metaverse, visiting sites, meeting new people, going to the movies, learning, and playing will be easier. You can do pretty much anything! You can bring the real world to the metaverse and, also metaverse to the real world. During the speech, Mark Zuckerberg announced the change of the company's name from Facebook to Meta. He explained that he intended on Meta being at the forefront in taking metaverse to the next step. He wanted a world where people could socialize and feel the experience no matter the distance and the part of the world they come from. He further explained that his number one goal is to produce AR glasses that would be used as the metaverse. He also pointed out that billions of dollars were channeled into the program to succeed. According to Zuckerberg, for metaverse to be fully operational, it would take some time and plenty of work. He also mentioned that he is aiming at leading the technology and will be using Meta's Quest AR headsets which will be its future. What are the features of the Quest? When you put on your headset, this will be the first thing that will appear. Horizon Home aims to help the user to be able to join games with friends, hang out, watch videos, and participate in games such as avatars. These activities will be done virtually. Since Covid 19 struck the entire world, companies have embraced the idea of employees working from home, and as we have seen, this idea is here to stay. Meta sees the future in virtual office space. With metaverse, doing presentations, attending the meeting, making coffee, and not to mention, the awkward office chit chat that happens would be made possible without physical interaction. Horizon Worlds will ensure everything you think of will be possible including performing your daily activities in the comfort of your home. Education plays an important role in the world. It is through education that inventions have been made. Metaverse aims at improving this sector. How cool will it be "traveling" to China to see the Great Wall, visiting the Vatican museums in Italy, and visiting the moon all through augmented reality? This will be a huge boost to the education sector, more so for students who prefer a visual experience when learning. Meta has set aside 150 million dollars to train the next generation to assist them in creating educational content. This move will therefore see the creation of a new curriculum and certification process of the program which will be easier to monetize. It is no doubt metaverse was created mainly for social purposes. Mark Zuckerberg, however, wants to ensure that you can make money out of this experience. So, how will it be possible? We've seen tremendous growth in the ecosystem over the years, and with this change, Meta is planning to use business ideas when building the metaverse. They sell their devices at lower prices to ensure that they are readily available to everyone. Zuckerberg believes that transforming metaverse into reality will be possible if we all work together. He also points out that within 10 years, billions of people will have joined metaverse. The main goals of the metaverse are to create innovations, interact with people, and create a business without physical appearance. I can only imagine how amazing it will be for you to order groceries only for them to be delivered to your doorstep with digital goods that you will be able to store in your virtual world. It might take a couple of years for metaverse to be in full operation as it is still in development. With that said, there is nothing to be done right now. But it is advisable to have a team ready to jump right into action when the development is complete. We've noticed that companies that tend to be the first to experience a new technology often have a lot to gain. Since this new technology will be offering courses and certificates after training, it is good to ensure that you prepare your team earlier. In this case, it will save you a lot of trouble and time-wasting when the development is complete. Also, companies that would have embraced AR/VR would have a better chance of getting involved with metaverse. Finally, introducing this new technology to your brand will be a game-changer for your business. Preparing early for the change will make a huge difference when metaverse development is complete. When asked how he tells his kids to prepare for the future of working with artificial intelligence, Peter Norvig said, "I tell them... Wherever they will be working in 20 years probably doesn't exist now. No sense training for it today. Be flexible," he said, "and can learn new things. Future of work experts and AI scientists believe that in the future there will be less full-time traditional jobs that require a single skill set, less routine administrative tasks, and less repetitive manual tasks—many jobs, then, will be all about "thinking" machines. From managers to janitors, everyone will adopt new ways of doing their jobs with machines in the next 20 years or so to come. One issue that is not clear, however, is whether the technological revolution will create more employment opportunities than it will destroy. According to Al Toby Walsh, copying

(Al computer) code costs almost zero and takes as much time. He goes on to say that whoever thinks technology will create more job opportunities than it will destroy is lying to themselves because nobody knows for sure. The jobs that AI will create will be different from the ones that will be destroyed, and they will require entirely different skills. Hamilton Calder, CEO of Committee for Economic Development Australia, thinks that everyone should learn to code. However, Mr. Charlton disagrees strongly. He is confident that you need not compete with machines to be successful in the future economy. Professor Walsh argues that, even though machines will be far better coders than humans, for geeks, there is a great future in inventing the future. It is time that people stopped encouraging the young generation to work towards a 'dream' job, says CEO of FYA, Jan Owen. Nobody should focus on an individual job. Instead, people should aim at developing a transferable skill set which includes digital and financial literacy, project management, collaboration, and the ability to carefully evaluate and analyze information. Robert Hillard, a managing partner at Deloitte Consulting, believes that future work will be divided into three categories. People who will work for machines like online store pickers and drivers. People will work with machines like surgeons who will be using the help of machines to diagnose. People who will work on machines like designers and programmers. The human-machine teams will unite AI algorithms with human skills like emotional intelligence and judgment. According to Mr. Hillard, jobs will increase, but they probably will not be better. Those that will be working for the machines will have the most difficult time. Yes, being human is a skill that you could leverage for income. Computers barely have emotional intelligence. The social jobs that need emotional intelligence (marketing jobs, being a nurse, being a psychologist) are safe. In the future, being human could be a job by giving services that machines cannot give—services in the caring economy, such as being empathetic. Some of these unpaid volunteering jobs could become "service jobs of love" in future. Computers are not creative or imaginative. Surprisingly, some of the oldest jobs ever, like being an artisan or a carpenter will be the most valuable ones. People would rather see something carved by a human as opposed to a machine. Even with all the preparedness for future work, Mr. Dawson thinks that everyone should plan for themselves. Develop the skills that will be needed and always pay attention.

Chapter 1
History of the Metaverse

We are living in a world that is advancing daily. And as we all can attest; the world is evolving around the metaverse. People are now open to the idea of having a decentralized society where the users are given the freedom to make their own choices. Today, cryptocurrencies and non-fungible tokens are exchanged freely. Through metaverse, we can be able to connect with people from all over the world. This brings us to the question: how did metaverse originate? Snow Crash and How It Influenced the Formation of the Metaverse - The word metaverse was first used in 1992 by Neil Stephenson in the sci-fi novel Snow Crash. This book later became an inspiration to the likes of Jeff Bezos, Mark Zuckerberg, and Sergey Brin in their effort to bring the virtual and physical worlds together. Metaverse can also be traced to have been used in the 20th century where several discoveries were made. It is through metaverse discovery that the world wide web which plays an important role in today's world was developed. We can socialize, do business with each other and not to mention learn from each other through this technology. Originally, it was mostly used by game developers and internet companies for their enterprises. These enterprises created the framework of virtual worlds like Fortnite, There, and Facebook Horizon. Though they were at the top of their game at the time, they lacked interconnectivity. Currently, the technology surrounding the metaverse has changed and there is so much to be offered to players compared to when it began. New players have been developed to match the corporate players that have dominated these games. Computer games were discovered a couple of decades ago. It is during this new millennium that games that allowed players to interact and play with each other were invented. These games became more popular in no time. Companies like There, RuneScape, and Second Life became exceedingly popular in the Metaversal gaming world. Later, a series of other games that would be seen to gain more followers emerged. Unfortunately, with the upcoming of new games that have more cool features, companies like Roblox, Minecraft, Fortnite, and Animal Crossing: New Horizon are losing their popularity. While these games offer social interaction, create businesses, and provide learning opportunities in the virtual world, they are still controlled by their developers. Meaning you cannot move from one game to another. For example, if you want to move from Animal Crossing to Fortnite then Zwift, it's going to be impossible as developers of these games have their own rules barring players from this move. From the success of these games, it is safe to say that metaverse has already taken the shape of its course. But how has this been achieved?

1998 A virtual world is developed where users can interact with each other, purchase and sell items using their currencies called "bucks". 2001 On this year RuneScape released massively multiplayer online role-playing game (MMORPG) 2003 Linden Lab Launches "second life" Its main aim is to create a platform where users can socialize and conduct business. 2006 Roblox, an online video game launch. 2011 There, comes back after it closed in 2010. 2012 RuneScape viewers reach $200 million. 2013 Oculus launches his prototype, Kickstarter Backer. 2014 A cycling game called immersive developed by Zwift is released. 2017 Fortnite Battle Royale, a free online game is released by its developer Epic Games. 2018-2019 Fortnite earns over $9billion in revenue. 2019 It is estimated that Roblox users who create items for purchase by other users can earn as high as $110million 2020 Animal Crossing Launches New Horizon that enables players with flora, fauna to interact with each other in a virtual world. 2020 Viewers of 'second life' reaches 1 million. 2021 Minecraft reaches 140million monthly users.

2021 The Republic of Korea announces that it will be launching a "National Metaverse Alliance" that will introduce a new platform of VR and AR. The novel 'Snow Crash' did not only introduce the universe to the metaverse, but it also left an impact on some of the best Silicon Valley pioneers such as Sergey Brin the cofounder of Google, Jeff Bezos the cofounder of Amazon, and Blue Origin founder.

The novel opened a door for new opportunities, these founders provided the environment for more companies to embrace metaverse. The significance of metaverse was seen in 2020 when the world was struck by Coronavirus where communication through the virtual world became the new normal. 2021 has seen significant growth in the usage of virtual reality as a means of communication. Companies like Zoom, Google, Microsoft, and other companies have seemingly seen an increase in their users since the pandemic. Since most of these platforms are still centralized, Microsoft is developing a platform where users will be able to interact virtually across devices (The Microsoft Mesh project). Where the rights and ownership will still be under Microsoft. This raises an eyebrow as to whether these apps will ever achieve decentralization. But how did Snow Crash inspire the future of the metaverse? 2000 The Cofounder of google Sergey Brin during an interview with the Academy of Achievement explained how the novel inspired the making of his company. 2000 Jeff Bezos recruited the author of Snow Crash to be part of Blue Origin which is the suborbital spaceflight. 2001 Memex (Cronin Blaise) is introduced by Microsoft. 2014 Facebook scientist Dean Eckles explained that Snow Crash was a book he would recommend project managers of social media platforms to read. 2014 Facebook spends $ 2.3 billion in purchasing Oculus 2020 During this year, the number of google video participants increased to 100 million daily. 2021 There was an increase in users of google from 115 million daily users to 145 million users. 2021 Mesh was developed. This project was meant to link users across devices. 2021 Facebook announces to CNET that one of its main objectives was to attract as many people as possible who will experience virtual reality. Early signs of the decentralized era first appeared in the 2000s and 2010. Colored coins which were the signs of a metaverse world began to gain popularity. The coins were used to create, purchase, and sell items that were unique to players. Although the colored coins could not be compared to other projects that were later developed, they opened the door to the world of the metaverse. The rise of NFTs games saw the beginning of a new era of NFT art that led Cryptokitty to sell over $170,000 in 2018. The unification of both blockchain and metaverse created a platform in the online universe where users connected and interacted virtually. How was these achieved? 2005 New serves were introduced by RuneScape which would see individuals manage their games as compared to the original version which was owned by Jagex. 2012 Yoni Assia first mentioned the colored coins. He explained that the coins brought a new world where users could buy and sell their items virtually. 2014 Counterparty introduced Bitcoin blockchain which allowed its users to trade currencies and items. 2017 Crypopunks creates 10,000 NFTs characters with each Cryptopunks having its unique features. 2017 Crypokitties is launched. This video game allows its users to collect, breed, and sell kittens. Surprisingly in 2018, a Crypokitty called Dragon sold at $172,000. 2021 Sotheby's holds NFTs art show that replicates the London galleries in a Decentraland metaverse. 2021 The album 'When You See Yourself' is released. Becoming the first album as an NFT to be released. The origin of the metaverse dates to the 20th century. After the release of the novel Snow Crash, founders of internet companies Amazon, Facebook and Google were influenced by the book and wanted to turn it into a reality so the competition to take the metaverse to the next level began. More platforms are being advanced to ensure all the user's imaginative ideas are being met. Everyone is on the lookout to see what is next!

Chapter 2
Crypto

Cryptocurrency is a virtual or digital type of currency that is meant for use as a means of exchange. These currencies are essentially a database of limited entries that someone cannot change until they meet conditions. The currency uses cryptography, which helps in securing as well as verifying transactions, not to mention controlling how new cryptocurrency units are created. The creation of cryptocurrency goes back to the 90s, where several systems entered the market but did not prevail. Fraud and financial constraints, as well as employees and employers, were some of the factors that led to the inevitable failure of such companies. Third party role-players took care of verification and staffing of transactions. After the companies failed miserably, the use of this system sank into the abyss for a long time, only to emerge around 2009 when electric peer-to-peer cash systems appeared in the market. This was all thanks to the Satoshi Nakamoto Bitcoin system, which was free from control by central authority. The same concept has held on to this day with other systems joining. Mining is essentially a significant aspect of cryptocurrency, which is an investment as well. Miners help with computing power for confirmation of transactions, as well as bookkeeping, which goes a long way to enhancing the efficiency of the network. Perhaps the most interesting thing about mining is that since it is about solving puzzles, the increasing number of people trying to solve it makes it more complex, which increases with the popularity of any of the digital currencies. These currencies can do quite a lot, with a wide array of purposes. Unlike the case in the past few years, some merchants online, as well as offline, are accepting Bitcoin as a form of payment. You can use the cryptocurrency to buy apps, book hotels, flights, and in bars as well as restaurants. Alternative cryptocurrencies like Ethereum, Ripple, and Litecoin have not become so popular yet, but there is a potential acceptance in the future for these types as well. The good news is that even though buying items with these other coins can be hectic, owners can always exchange their coins for Bitcoin and still get whatever they need. And with most sellers and websites alike increasingly accepting this type of currency, it is just a matter of time multiple digital currencies in the market will be as useful. Bitcoin has increased in popularity and value. Ethereum is coming in second at a fast-paced price increase. But remember that as lucrative as these currencies may seem, investing in them is a risky business as it is the case with trading and any other investment. Cryptocurrencies have travelled a long way and are developing even further by the day. And while the business might seem promising, it is worth noting that legality of the currencies might differ in countries around the world, and the currencies come in a wide range of varieties, so it all comes down to what you want to work with or the rules in your location. As the use of blockchain gains popularity, the system has seen its fair share of hype over the years, and more research has been directed at looking into the appropriateness of this technology. Thanks to the creation of authorization and authentication of different processes in the digital world, it has ruled out the need for the use of centralized administrators. This efficiency has eventually created an upsurge of digital relationships, hence leading layers of the internet ideal for the performance interactions and transactions of values. The new tech, also known as the "internet of value" is apparently overriding the "internet of information" that has been in place for the last few decades. However, this new internet layer does come with several downsides as well, which will make cryptographic keys, blockchain, and cryptocurrencies an unfavorable option eventually. So where is the line between which of the two models is the best? Well, the use of paper has been efficient, thanks to the fact that it is hard to counterfeit with all the seals and appearances among other factors. But this can be a difficult approach when you consider a constant and regular flow of transactions since the method may not be ideal if someone wants to keep up the pace. Besides, manual data entry comes with its challenges as well. The flexibility of blockchain, as well as the ability to cater to the wide range of parties writing entries, can be beneficial. In most cases, third-party participants play a vital role in taking care of authorizations and authentication of transactions. This can be useful if security is the focus, but when the privacy of the data outweighs all else, there is no need for connecting it to any network for security reasons. This is where blockchain comes into play, offering the ideal security for the digital identity that would otherwise be impossible. In case a database must support lightweight financial transactions, blockchain can be rather useful. Another inevitable consideration is the transaction speed. If speed is the key, in which case transactions should be carried out in milliseconds and yet with high performance, a centralized system will be the way to go. The drawback for blockchain is relatively slow and storing the data comes with a cost. But with the centralized data systems that feature a client-server operation, speed is attainable, and they are not expensive. This gives the centralized models an upper hand over blockchain. The bottom line is that as much as the potential of blockchain is yet to be fully unveiled, most of the areas that have been confirmed to be useful so far include the aspect of securing as well as managing digital-based relationships. This can benefit as a system record, but slightly fails when it comes to the performance and speed in carrying out transactions. But with these systems developing by the day, only time can tell when they will become a cutting-edge solution. For now, only the participant can decide on what is best for them in carrying out such transactions. Better yet, the tech is also packing enough potential up its sleeve to transform the conventional business model in multiple sectors. Essentially, these chains work on a similar idea with large digital spreadsheets that all members in a decentralized network can access. The great thing about blockchain is that although it is well known for its use in bitcoin transactions, this technology has other uses as well. And with the increasing value of bitcoin and its dominance in several mainstream sectors, companies offering financial services are stepping into the action. One of the things that make cryptocurrency a darling for most people is the currency's ability to cut back on the costs incurred in the transfer of funds especially when it comes to sending money across borders. While some investors are opting to stockpile gold and wait for the value to skyrocket, you can take advantage of the potential increase in the price of bitcoin. Although bitcoin is not as tangible as gold, the investment principles for both are similar. The supply and demand balance is the key here, and with the two being rare, you can step in on the opportunity to invest. Pure blockchain tech play is gaining traction by the day, with numerous companies taking part in this sector becoming increasingly popular. One of the widely known companies, BTCS, is renowned as the premier "pure play" company in the US to focus on the use of blockchain technology. It works through unique verification services for transactions to make blockchain secure. Another company that is also gaining popularity is Global Arena Holding, which is enhancing blockchain technology in the potential of the tech for enabling voter verification. Angel funding has been around for a while now, but the idea of using startups in blockchain is giving it a completely new outlook. Bitcoin has become popular, and everyone is looking into getting a share of the action, but this comes with funding. Well, with angel funding, you can be able to venture into the technology and stand to benefit from the innovation that it has to offer in the future. Another interesting idea for blockchain is with penny stocks, which include other types of cryptocurrencies like Altcoins such as Algorand. Most of these coins were designed to help in ways where bitcoins are not applicable but were primarily meant to pose a healthy competition for the popular cryptocurrency. If you are looking into raising capital for any investment, there is no better way to do so than with the use of crowdfunding, which has become the primarily used and popular method for this purpose. You can use this to invest in blockchain, thanks to the use of alternative coins, or altcoins, which are pre-mined and sold in an initial coin offering, also known as ICO. This is carried out before the public launching of the network. Among the most popular methods is the use of bit shares. With these options at your disposal, only your choice matters now. However, it is worth considering risk as well and make sure you minimize risks to the lowest levels possible. If there is one certain thing about blockchain, it is the fact that these are revolutionized systems of records. Since the time it was invented as the world's premier decentralized and permanent ledger-based records, entrepreneurs have understood its implications. But blockchain has also seen its fair share of speculations as well, considering that the idea is applicable in virtually anything to do with records. This concept is ruling out the need for authorities to oversee transactions since cryptography gives individuals the power to do this all by themselves. The hype about these chains is centered on the probability of high-level use circumstances where blockchain tech can be applied. Digital identity can help as a system of records with the use of cryptographic keys, which allows individuals to have the right and means to form digital relationships with others. This comes from the fact that the concept doesn't rely on accounts or permissions related to accounts, the security in managing identity in the digital realm is relatively secure. And it is all thanks to the fact that one is not exposed to sharing excessive personal information that can be compromised. Another means in which this technology proves valuable is when used as a platform. This usually comes down to some of its top-of-the-line aspects like its use for automated governance and smart contracting. Besides, it can also help with streamlining clearances and settlement in stock trading. Another area where this tech is applicable is in automation of regulatory compliance using the code form in governments' legal systems. Data management also plays a major role in gathering and collection of information for governments. This usefulness has seen governments develop an interest in three components of the technology. One of the things that make it ideal is the rights associated with ownership, generation, and revocation, replacing, or losing the cryptographic keys. There is also some interest associated with the aspect of who can participate in any chain, as well as interest in protocols based on blockchain when it comes to authorization of transactions. As such, many blockchain developers believe that regulatory compliance offers a potential business opportunity. The use of paring items with their corresponding digital tokens also comes in quite handy for authentication of physical items. Therefore, tokens can be used to bridge both the physical as well as the digital sides. As such, tokens are used in the management of supply chains as well as control of intellectual property, fraud detection, and anti-counterfeiting detection. Banks, as well as other financial institutions, usually rely on client-server infrastructure to run individual accounts. But keeping it secure from hackers can be a daunting task, especially with the risk of hacking at any given time. With blockchain technology, however, these institutions can create an automatically developed record of who can access records or information. Besides, they can also take control regarding permissions to access information.

Chapter 3
Metaverse Blockchain

Ledgers have been around for years, if money and the art of writing have been in the life of humanity. From clay to wooden tally sticks, papyrus, and paper, ledgers have come a long way through history. And with the emergence of computers in the 1980s and 1990s, paper records went digital, usually through data entry by manual work. These include the changes that ledgers have seen in the past. Digital ledgers of the contemporary world resemble the accounting and cataloging of the old days of paperwork. It is, however, apparent that digitization has been used significantly on the logistics concerning paper documents than it has been done on the creation of paperwork. Nevertheless, paper-related institutions are still the mainstream of today's society. Talk of written signatures, seals, money certificates, bills as well as double-entry bookkeeping and other similar uses of paper documented records. But despite the tight grip of papers on society, distributed ledgers have been created, thanks to the discovery and use of interesting new algorithms. Besides, advances in cryptography and computing power have also played a significant role in making this development real. In essence, distributed ledgers involve a database that is held in a massive network and continuously updated independently by isolated participants, also known as nodes within the network. Each distribution is separate, in which case the records are constructed independently and retained by each of the nodes. This process is done instead of the information being communicated to the nodes by any central authority. This means every given node in the system processes each transaction and achieves its conclusions, and then the conclusions are voted on to ascertain agreement by the majority. Upon achieving consensus, the distributed ledger is then updated, with every single node maintaining a ledger's copy that is identical across the board. This method offers a new mode of using record systems that outperforms the use of simple databases. Perhaps the best part about these ledgers is the fact that they are dynamic, with capabilities and properties that outperform the static paper ledger design. This achievement makes the new ledgers ideal for enabling users to formalize as well as securing new relationships that can be far reaching in the computer world. These relationships help keep the cost of trust at bay, thanks to the architecture and the qualities that these ledgers offer. Therefore, newly distributed ledgers are a revolution in communication and information. This aspect applies to the static data, which is a registry, as well as the dynamic data, represented by the transactions. As such, these ledgers allow users to achieve more than just simple manipulation of databases, helping divert energy from the use, extraction, and manipulation of value from databases. Not to mention, the benefits further accrue to the maintenance of databases as well as management of record systems. Apparently, ledgers have moved to another level, thanks to the computerization of the process, and the advantages of new technology are outstanding. The system of blockchain technology is not a complicated one; it is all about three major principal technologies, which make the chain. This technology includes a distributed network, a private key cryptography, and an incentive for servicing transactions in the network as well as keeping records and ensuring security. With blockchain, a network serves the purpose of helping validators identify a particular event, usually one that was witnessed by multiple people at the same time. Although the reason behind the change might be unclear, the most important thing is having noticed that nothing happened in the first place. In such cases, the size of the network goes a long way to securing it in the long term. Cryptographic keys are essential for creating a digital reference for security in blockchain. The digital identity in this case means a combination of both a public as well as a private cryptographic key owned by the user. Together, the two keys make a digital signature that someone can use to access their blockchain without compromising the security of others or jeopardizing their own safety. But securing the access is not as simple; the transactions and permissions need to be put in check as well. The combination of both approaches is useful in making a tight security for everyone. Record system is the combination of the cryptographic keys and the use of a network. And this is where digital interactions come into play. In such instances, one person takes their private key and announces that they are sending a certain amount of the cryptocurrency to another person. This is especially applicable in the case of bitcoin blockchain. Then there is the protocol, where the relevant information and digital signature as well as timestamp are then distributed to every node in the network. For some people, the thought of having to amass computer power to secure a network through servicing might not be as practical. In essence, the idea comes from the need to bring together numerous computers, where someone's interest is used to serve the need for many, while the individual is rewarded for their input. Network servicing protocol in bitcoin is meant to get rid of any possibility for the same bitcoin being used in different transactions at once in an undetectable way. In this way, the currency seeks to act as a property, especially gold. The verification, as well as amount and type, can differ in separate blockchain technology; it all depends on the protocol for the chain. This is also known as the rules governing what transaction is valid and what isn't, besides, they also determine the validity of the creation of any block. The verification can also differ depending on the blockchain since the creation of any necessary incentives or rules can be achieved provided there are enough nodes who agree on how to verify the transactions. The process in which these chains operate might sound complex, but it is quite straightforward. All it takes is considering the aspects that govern what should be carried out and what is to be left alone. Once you understand the basics, you can jump right into the action and take part in the implementation of the technology right from your computer. Public and Permissioned Blockchains comprise of three technologies, which include a distributed network, cryptography keys, as well as network servicing protocol. One of the leading types of blockchain is Bitcoin. Users can utilize its cryptographic keys, and any of the users can be a node and be able to join the vast network. And there is more; anyone can also earn revenue by becoming a miner to servicing the network. More interestingly, anyone can stop being a node and come back whenever they want and still get a full account of the entire network activity from the time left. In essence, someone can study the chain; carry out legitimate changes, or even write a new block in the chain. The great thing about Bitcoin is that it is decentralized, and further termed as a "censor-proof" chain. This means the chain is popular for its widest description as a public chain. However, this does not point out the only way someone can build a blockchain. Another blockchain that can be built are the ones requiring permission to access the information on the chain. In this case, the parties who can transact on the chain are limited, and the users who can write new blocks in the chain and serve the network. One example of permission blockchain is Ripple's chain. It is up to the startup to determine whether and who can validate a transaction on the blockchain network. These blockchain transaction validators so far are MIT, CGI, and Microsoft, but it is further building its nodes in several locations around the world. Besides, a developer can decide to avail the system of record to everyone for reading. But one can also choose whether to make anyone a node with the ability to serve the security of the network, as well as whether the node can carry out mining or transaction verification. It all comes down to a mix-and-match scenario that depends on various means of entrepreneurs doing experiments on the technology. In the case of permission blockchain, this method might not have anything to do with proof of the work or any other requirements in the system. The aspect is still a matter of discussion, with some people considering private chains as not being blockchain at all, due to the lack of proof of use as well as mining. Some think, these are just shared ledgers rather than blockchain. However, despite the different perceptions on blockchain, it is all about making the most out of your chain with the ultimate control, whether in a permission or public chain. It all comes down to managing your blockchain the best way to get the most benefits out of it. Blockchain technology follows a quite simple rule, which is a combination of three technologies that make up the chain. These come down to the network servicing protocol, cryptographic keys, as well as a distributed network. These technologies are the underlying factors in almost any aspect of this platform, even the cryptocurrencies such as bitcoin work on this principle. In the case of bitcoin, the leading ambitious type of blockchain, the concept is virtually the same all the way. Not forgetting, a user can also become a miner since anyone can play this role to service the network and earn rewards. Perhaps the best thing is that a node can shift from the role and return whenever they wish to. Better yet, when a user returns, they can still find a track of all the activity in the account for the entire time they have been on the other side. Blockchain is designed in a way that anyone can do virtually anything to the network, from just reading, to making legitimate changes, and even adding a new block to the chain, provided the user sticks to the rules. This is all thanks to the decentralized nature of blockchain, especially Bitcoin, also referred to as a "censor-proof" blockchain. This design and structure make bitcoin a perfect example of a public blockchain. However, this type of system is not the only way in which public chains operate. Nevertheless, the nature of blockchain has seen a fair share of discussion as well, with some people thinking that chains that do not involve mining should not be termed as blockchain since they are just shared ledgers. The technology surrounding these chains can be quite complex, but when you leave out the mathematical algorithms, and other complicated stuff, and focus on the layout and the three basic principles, it becomes easy to understand. For the last two years, blockchain and non-fungible tokens (NFT) have been at the top of the chats when it comes to technology. In every 5 Britons, 1 is sure that investing in NFT is a good investment. And in the United States, at least 18 percent of the population has invested in NFT. NFT is digital data or art that is not easily plagiarized or replaced. They use blockchain to store their ledger. Lately, the number of blockchain users has been increasing. In a recent study that was conducted by Deloitte, several people were convinced that digital currencies would replace the normal currency in the next coming years. As we know, investment in blockchain and NFT has been physical and in terms of monetary value. But after Facebook announced the launching of metaverse on their platform, the perception of metaverse changed. Also, cryptocurrencies like Mana that traded on the digital world saw a 400% rise in their users from Facebook's launch of the metaverse. The big question is what Facebook's plan on blockchain for the metaverse. For you to get a clear picture of how blockchain works on metaverse, let's have a look at it. Blockchain is a digital ledger that stores all the information electronically in a digital format. This ledger contains a list of records or blocks that are linked through cryptography techniques. The records have mathematical algorithms that describe the next block on the chain, the time it was accessed, and any other transaction made. And for this reason, they can't be copied or hacked. The security of this technology is tight as their network operates on the peer-to-peer network. The PCs share files and access to devices such as printers without requiring an external server. Blockchain can be used for many purposes which include monitoring logistics, recording health records, anti-money laundering, and as an archive for the music. As we all know, cryptocurrencies are digital assets that are traded online by a decentralized network. This network operates through blockchain. Just like any other currency, you can use blockchain to purchase anything you want. Also, they vary from time to time as no agency controls or regulates its value. Currently, the number of cryptocurrencies has increased from decades ago. Now we have Bitcoin, Ethereum, Mana just to name a few. Let's look at how blockchain and metaverse relate. What Comes into Your Mind When We Talk of Metaverse and Blockchain? The metaverse is a digital platform where users can interact with each other socially and in terms of business. This platform is unique for these reasons; it cannot be plagiarized, it is infinite, self-sufficient, and not to mention decentralized. Now let's imagine a metaverse that uses cryptocurrencies, how cool will that be! A digital world that is not bothered by the real world and its environment whether physical or in terms of value. As we have seen earlier, the metaverse has a decentralized economy and no one can control the metaverse. Decentralizing the currency ensures that people adhere to the same rule. With the constant technological change, these currencies can be a useful factor in bringing together the current world and the future world. The idea of the metaverse was to allow ideas to become a reality. The developers of these metaverses ensure their users experience the real world but in virtual reality. With blockchain having been introduced to the metaverse, the stability of this philosophy is instilled. When in-game assets are allowed to be NFTs that can be bought and sold then virtual reality will become a platform that can earn you real money in the virtual world. Assets would remain un interfered with even in the case where a user quits the game, or the game was deleted. As the technology surrounding the metaverse keeps evolving, blockchain can act as a social security number but virtual. Your employees, their age, and your account transactions can be recorded on the blockchain not only for security but also to keep a track record of every event that takes place in the metaverse. As mentioned earlier in our previous chapters, real estate is a booming business in the metaverse. Regulating real estate is not an easy task due to its infinite nature. You can use blockchain to keep all the records regarding how real estate is created, traded, and destroyed in the metaverse. In every game, there is always that person who does not want to play by the rules. And the metaverse is no different. Last August, Epic Games sued Apple for charging a 30% fee for every purchase made of their items through Epic

Game's popular platform Fortnite. Blockchain will ensure that users of the currencies abide by the rules by recording the contracts made. This will in turn ensure fair governance of the currencies. During the rebranding of Facebook to Meta, Mark Zuckerberg announced his plan to introduce metaverse to his technology. He stated that his metaverse will be based on privacy, open standards, and safety. He also added that a new form of governance had to be implemented.

Unfortunately, he did not mention Meta's plans for blockchain. However, Facebook has its currency called Libra that was introduced in 2019 that later changed its name to Novi then finally Diem. Facebook has placed all the necessary materials for the introduction of metaverse on its platform. All we can do is wait and see what they have in store for us when the project is complete.

Chapter 4
The Metaverse and Artificial Intelligence

Artificial intelligence is gaining tremendous capabilities by the day, but for some, this can be a significant threat to our future. Some of the issues highlighted surrounding AI are the implementation of the technology and the other involves its regulation. One of the major risks for machine learning and AI is the deployment of technology for the wrong purpose, which will lead to unfairness and bias against society. Experts have already warned against the rapid adoption of artificial intelligence, in several fields like education and prison sentencing among others. The biggest problem is the fact that predictive models can hardly be neutral. Hence, they only represent the interests of the people who create them and work against the poor, and the result is utter inequality. Algorithms are increasingly becoming a part of our daily lives. They determine numerous aspects such as news feed on Facebook, online ads, and determining credit ratings as well as job applications among other functions. It is thus important to ensure we test these machines beforehand to avoid biases that can come from both historical data and the data fed into the machines. But regulating technology as of now remains uncharted, and this is where blockchain will come into the play. Thanks to a significant role that blockchain can implement in regulating AI technologies and machine learning, it can prove worthy for society when all else has failed. The tamper-proof way of keeping records makes it an ideal measure for regulation on autonomous artificial intelligence areas. Besides, blockchain technology can help with controlling the access of any of the autonomous artificial intelligence entities depending on the agent's reputation. The best way to deal with an AI entity is to put it completely out of commission, or if you are not in the position to do so, then you can deter public access altogether. If you look at it from a philosophical point of view, the best description of the phenomenon is the argument by Thomas Hobbes, an English philosopher who suggested that citizens should be ready to give up part of their power to an isolated ruler for the benefit of the society. This option still has not been tested and much has not been written on the effect of the leviathan search engine proposed by Hobbes to control machine learning and AI. In case this approach is put in place, the use of AI leviathan will enable pushing autonomous agents controlled by blockchain through identification as well as reporting. Perhaps the best input about blockchain is the immunity, which makes it secure from any interruption by any of the agents, society will have a reputable ledger that can cover all autonomous artificial intelligence agents. As such, the Leviathan approach will be an effective policing technology on the agreed rules and carry out sanctions if necessary. It is thus clear that the creation of blockchain is one of the best ways through which society can establish an unbiased and equitable approach to multiple aspects affecting everyday life. For years, ledgers have been around as the basis for accounting, a form that has been in use for as long as money and writing have existed. Ledgers have come down from the days of clay and wooden sticks to papyrus, stone, paper, and then computers took over late in the 20th century. Once the computers took over, ledgers were digitized, usually using manual data entry. But one thing remains for sure; the concept is still the same all along. Years ago, involving digital ledgers, the process was carried out more like the case with accounting and cataloging before the digital revolution, so digitization took more of the logistics applied in the paper ledgers than focusing on a new way of creation. Paper and its related institutions remain a significant and inevitable part of our society. From written signatures to money, seals, certificates, and bills as well as double entry bookkeeping, it's all part of everyday life. The development of cryptography and the new use of algorithms have brought a new dawn to the basics of ledgers, the distributed ledgers. In simple terms, a distributed ledger is a database that is operated and updated by isolated participants, also known as nodes, which are combined to form a vast network. The basic factor here is that there is no use of any central authority in charge of communicating records to the nodes. Rather, every node constructs and maintains a record independently. This means every node in the chain can carry out a transaction, then check through the conclusions to ensure that the majority are in consensus with any conclusion. The consensus on any transaction means the ledger is updated, so every single node keeps a copy of that ledger. This design makes the distributed ledger stay a step ahead of the simple conventional database, thanks to the high level of record keeping. Distributed ledgers can be seen as dynamic media forms whose capabilities and properties outweigh the use of static paper ledgers of the old days, and this is what gives blockchain a leverage and high potential as a system. Thanks to the effectiveness of the system, users can formalize and keep new relationships secure in a perilous digital world where hackers are looming in every corner. With this unique structure, distributed ledgers go beyond just offering opportunities and security, to helping cut costs involved in trust-related processes like banks, lawyers, and notaries among others. The new development in the world of ledgers, which has seen distributed ledgers take the entire concept of record keeping to a new height, bringing a completely new way in the methods of gathering and communicating information. Perhaps what makes ledgers a greater option is the ability to help with static data, also known as a registry, as well as in the case of dynamic data, which involves transactions. The bottom line, users can move beyond the confines of database's simple custodianship, to venture out to new ways of manipulating and extracting value from these databases. Eventually, rather than working to maintain a database, we can instead manage a system of records that offer more benefits in the long run. Blockchain has numerous benefits to offer in different sectors of society, and one of its major advantages is offering security for data, ensuring the elimination of common fraud cases by hackers, and enhancing security for financial services. Also, offering a much-needed security for financial relationships for businesses and individuals across the globe. As the co-author of Blockchain Revolution, Alex Tapscott points out; blockchain technology is more like the case for the internet back in 1993, where no one took notice of the potential of the revolution. Many people have heard about the revolution, but only a few have made a move to try it. The trend may be attributed to the fact that the technology is quite complicated and technical to an extent due to the mathematical algorithms involved and digital protocol. What's more, it may also be due to the lack of extensive practical application in the tech world. And although it might be too complex for the layman, the basic idea comes down to a massive global-class ledger, which anyone at any place in the world can use to store, move, or manage any assets. These could be securities, money, intellectual property, and many others. Perhaps the best thing is that moving or manipulating these assets can be done securely and privately without necessarily having to involve any intermediaries such as the government or banks. As such, just as the internet was regarded to be the first medium for information, blockchain technology is described as a premier digital medium for value. Blockchain is termed as a window to opportunities that were previously impossible, thanks to its secure nature, which for some means it is impenetrable. Besides, the decentralized design makes this tech one of the best out there, since no one can claim ownership or manipulate it in any way, as would be the case with a centralized form. This makes blockchain different from other security systems, usually created by a particular person or company, or licensed to someone. As such, it means the system is sturdy against any loopholes where fraudsters may take advantage. In essence, to hack cryptocurrency in a blockchain, for instance, someone will require a computing power high enough to access every single computer linked to the ledger at the same time. This requirement means massive power, estimated to be up to the power of a hundred google machines, also known as googolian. Moreover, decentralized technology means there is no room for failure at any single point that can prove fatal to the entire system. The use of data structure blocks involves a timestamp as well as a link to the preceding block. Therefore, any transaction in the chain is traceable, but remains irreversible, perhaps one of the means to offer more security. These efficiencies are among the components that make blockchain so sturdy that will help drive society into the future. It is apparent that with time, this technology will unleash its full potential with far-reaching benefits for virtually everyone. According to experts, robots will be a part of life in 2025. These machines will be in our homes, stores, places of work, you name it. The only question that everyone is trying to answer is what this new change will leave in its wake as far as humanity is concerned, especially when it comes to the workplace. More than half the percentage is convinced that technology will not take over more human jobs than the ones tech will help create. That is fifty-two percent of people optimistic about machine intelligence transforming us for the better, with the other 48% still skeptical that this will spell doom for jobs and wages. The issue is still subject to confirmation and lengthy debate. But there is a catch since there is a possibility that most employers will still consider human labor for white and blue color jobs that machines can do well. According to the people who believe we are still safe from machine takeover; technology will still play the part it has always been part of from before. Machines will thus help in the improvement of productivity as well as creating the opportunity to focus on human jobs that require skills for problem-solving and advanced creativity. For others, however, this will remain a precarious economic rule whereby automation poses a significant risk to the increase of corporate profits and wages. Machines can carry out more intricate and complex tasks nowadays. This is all thanks to the advancing computer vision, sensors, ability to learn, and algorithm among other technical advances. According to an Oxford study, 45 percent of jobs in the U.S will most likely be automated in the period of two decades. However, experts have varying opinions concerning the threat that machine intelligence poses to humanity regarding work. One of the things that optimistic experts point out is the fact that automation has never posed any threat to reduce job opportunities in the economy so far, and the same is highly unlikely in the future. This is because automation helps reduce prices, hence increasing demand for services and goods, eventually creating jobs. The other factor that is termed reliable is the ability of automation to create more jobs than it can displace. This difference means there will always be enough jobs created in the process to ensure no lack of job results. Others say that the main risk to jobs is not necessarily AI, but large-scale shifts in employment to areas where labor is less expensive. And even though automation has been feared to take over human jobs for the past few decades, the real risk lies in the aspect of risk management rather than technology taking over human jobs. The experts who do not believe that this will not mean any threat to jobs have concerns over the versatility and always advancing capabilities of AI and robotics. They claim that this will not only affect numerous economic sectors but might extend to have effects on whole swaths. This comes down to economic efficiency, and the trend is already affecting some sectors. Others believe that automation processes that target the core of the economy will kick humans out as the shift takes effect. For some experts, only the most educated humans will stand a chance in the war for jobs against machines. These experts believe that the worst part is that students are not being well prepared for this change. As much as automation may seem like a threat to the survival of humanity as far as employment is concerned, it is important to remember that this technology can come with jobs never created. It is more about looking into the jobs that will be replaced in the future because bots were not able to create it and will be lost to machines. We live in a world that is advancing in terms of technology. A recent survey by McKinsey showed that at least 50% of the world's companies use AI. Another study by

Deloitte noted that 40% of most business entities had planned on using AI in the future. AI plays a vital role in the consumer-facing application. It provides instant consumer service in terms of mobile services, faster computing, and creating a fast interaction between the creator and the user. When metaverse was introduced, it was only a matter of time before AI began operating in the virtual worlds. They have the capability of storing a large amount of data and at a high speed. Also, they can help create an authentic sense of touch as well as aid in voice-enabled navigation. There is an expectation of the metaverse using the two worlds, that is, Augmented and Virtual Reality in conjunction with blockchain and artificial intelligence to transform virtual reality into a more sophisticated technology. Before we look at how the two technologies relate, let's look at the metaverse to get a clear understanding of how the two will work.

Metaverse is essentially the merging of virtual, augmented, and physical reality. The word metaverse was first introduced by a science fiction novelist known as Neil Stephenson in the early 90s. Later, companies such as Second Life, Decentraland, Microsoft, and the most recent Meta, joined in the development of the metaverse. Meta, which was initially Facebook is a company that is well known for the use of AI and the creation of AI algorithms. Their research teams are working on several projects which include speech processing, robotics interactions, whole-body pose estimation, and computer vision just to name a few. If all the projects they are working on are successful, Meta's future in the metaverse will have a positive impact. Metaverse can work independently even without AI. But a combination of the two will bring a new world of fun and opportunities to the metaverse. But how will this be achieved? When playing a video game, there are unique qualities that make you pick a certain character. You want a character that has the latest gears, ready to engage anything. In the metaverse, you will also require the best of these characters. An AI can analyze 2D user images and create what you wish your avatar character to be like. It can input facial expressions, hairstyle, emotion, and other external features brought about by the physical appearances of a person like the age to make your avatar as real as possible.

A company like Ready Player Me is working on developing AI that will be used in the metaverse. In June, Mark Zuckerberg announced that his company intended on adding metaverse to their technology. Digital humans are AI-powered human beings that offer a combination of both AI and humans. They can create a unique and dynamic experience for virtual world users. They are created entirely from AI technology and are vital in the shaping of the metaverse. AI in the metaverse can play various roles, they can be your automated VR assistant, create human emotion in your avatar, and be your brand ambassadors. Digital humans use AI to process information like language. An AI can listen to a speech, analyze it, and convert it to an understandable language called multilingual accessibility. Also, they can assist in solving a problem by listening to your issue and providing you with the solution. Another awesome feature it has is that it can convert the speech to any language which allows the players in the metaverse to communicate and play without any language barrier. Now, this is where things get more interesting! We all know that AI can store larger amounts of data. If for instance it is fed with historical data or events, it analyzes the data and tries to replicate the same event or data but in a more sophisticated and accurate way. With every data that it is fed, it will get better at analyzing and creating new VR environments. Eventually, it will be able to solve problems almost as humans. Companies like NVIDIA are training and inputting commands on their AI so that they can create VR worlds.

This new move will play an important role in the metaverse world expansion without the aid of humans. AI also provides a link of communication and interaction between computers and humans. If you put your headsets on and go into the metaverse, The AI can automatically sense from your behavior and previous patterns how you would like to move. When gaming, AI can create a sense of touch allowing players to experience the real world. Also, they can be created to have a voice recognition feature that allows you to give commands and navigate the metaverse without using your hands. The development of metaverse and AI are still on their primal stage and not many people fully understand the technology. With that said, some questions may arise. In some cases, issues to do with the copyrights may arise. Which Begs the question: who has the right to ownership of content in the metaverse? How do you assure your users that they are communicating with an AI and not just a fellow human? Can you assure your users they are playing a fair game, and no one has been handed over the AI codes to win the game? If a player has committed an offense. What is the course of action for that user? Lastly, it is hard to have the experience of your life in the metaverse without the aid of an AI. Features like natural language processing, creating human emotion, and navigating the metaverse without using your hand would be next to impossible. And it is for these reasons that a company like Meta is investing in AI.

Chapter 5
Meta Virtual Reality

The term virtual reality is almost self-explanatory. Virtual means almost or near while reality means what is experienced. Therefore, virtual reality fundamentally implies near-reality. It is used to refer to an imitation of reality. We know our reality or our world through our perception systems and our senses. All that we know is a combination of the information that our senses convey to the brain and how the brain makes sense of it. Thus, you can 'create' a reality by feeding the senses with fabricated information. This new reality that you will know is one that does not really exist, but you will perceive as if it does. Now that is virtual reality. Defining it in technical terms is easy. It is simply a three-dimensional environment created by a computer and can interact with and be explored by a person. The person can perform actions in that environment since they become a part of it. In today's world, virtual reality can be achieved by use of computer technology. Examples of systems that can be used to achieve this include special gloves, headsets, and omnidirectional treadmills. The systems provoke the senses together and achieve a misapprehension of reality. It sounds simple but it is not. Our brains are wired in such a way that, if anything is amiss, we will notice. Hence virtual reality technology considers the aspect of our physiology. It seeks to combine software, hardware, and sensory synchronicity perfectly to achieve the sense of presence. You may be wondering why someone would go through all that trouble. First, it is for entertainment purposes. The entertainment sector is a gold-mine. The uncountable consumers of this industry are very keen on newness. Virtual reality is also used in 'more serious' fields like: Medicine, Sports,

Architecture, and the Arts. One feature that is common to all of them is the fact that they can let one view a three-dimensional image. To this person, the images are life-sized. They also transform as the person navigates the environment. The virtual environment must provide suitable responses as the person moves around it. The responses must be in real time. If a delay occurs between the person's action and the response, then the experience is interrupted. The brain realizes that the environment is artificial. Virtual reality technology creates an artificial reality and allows someone to experience it as if they are really in it. It 'corrupts' the senses and brain into believing it. It is a complicated kind of technology that simplifies life. This technology is a big step into the future. Although it is complicated and not quite affordable, it is spreading quickly. It has brought a much-needed advancement in vital fields like medicine. Hopefully, it will lead to other great innovations that will make the globe an even smaller village. 2016 was a year intended for Virtual Reality. Thanks to great growth facilitators like Google, HTC, Samsung, and Oculus, it was. The technology enhanced fast enough. 2017 is now expected to be the year that VR rises. The market is now larger, and you can even earn a living from it. But how can you earn money from VR? If you are excited about VR and the potential opportunities of this new and amazing industry, then you are thrilled to combine passion and work and earn a living from it. Several VR enthusiasts from all over the world, each of them unique in their own way, brought to light the types of jobs that are there in the VR world. The following suggestions will be helpful to any ambitious person who is out to create a personal VR legacy. Take for example a developer who is talented in game engines such as Unreal or Unity. The first way to earn money would be to create and sell your own video game. How cool is that? You may not have the resources to build something like Job Simulator on your own, but you can build a game like Pinball pro-VR (a VR Pinball player) which was built by a single person. If you have built your game, there are two ways to monetize it: You can decide to sell it for free and probably monetize it by including advertising in your experience. You can find several startups in the market which can help you connect with brands. The other option is to put your game on the Oculus/Steam store and sell it for money. The store takes 30% commission so you will get 70% of your selling price. The first option may be the coolest and maybe easiest way of earning with VR. However, if you cannot code, setting up a simulation, game, or application on your own is not possible.

If you are creative and have marketing skills this option is for you. There are so many opportunities to advise corporations on VR. Many brand representatives are eager to create engagement through VR, but they have no idea how to approach it. They rarely have the time to collect information or even set up a VR system. You can make money by selling your wisdom to them. People in the VR industry are hungry for data. There is a lot of information they need to pitch their ideas to corporations. For example, they would like to know what really molds the feeling of presence or how a user navigates a digital environment. These are just a few ways, but they are great places to start. If you are a VR technology junkie, consider monetizing your passion. This is the time to start thinking about how you will create the next virtual game or how to advise a certain company, be a VR researcher and immerse yourself in something that you really love. Having your passion earn you money is a dream come true. Normally, the real estate industry changes with time and is quick to embrace technology to enhance its services. However, when it comes to Virtual Reality technology it seems to exhibit skepticism. Those that hesitate to adopt it could be making a grave mistake while those that do could be doing themselves a great favor. The two most common problems faced by real estate agents are: Having to manage time visiting one house after another, with obstacles like traffic making it even harder. Having to hear buyers say, "it doesn't look like the pictures" all the time. Virtual reality is the ultimate answer to these two issues. It makes it possible to virtually show many houses in a short time. This improves sales efficiency, allows an agent to attend to more buyers and show more houses. Look at the various ways you can use VR to improve your sales and make real estate a delight. Guided Virtual Visits is a lot more like a promotional video, but it is shot and produced in 360 degrees. It is an amazing method for existing properties. Real estate agents will also be able to show properties still under construction. It is possible to produce a virtual visit of an incomplete building by mixing several types of mediums in the virtual experience. By producing a high-quality 3D version of, say the bedroom, a buyer can have a clearer idea of how their future bedroom will look when it is completed. In the spirit of improving virtual visits, this experience can be even more interactive when movement is determined by the user. It is a mind-blowing experience for potential buyers. With almost everyone having heard of VR but to try it, this will be life changing. This experience will have to be accommodated in a mobile app. This experience is caused by hotspots that will appear in your field of vision whenever you shift your attention from one side to another. If you keep your sight on the hotspot, you will be transported to the hotspot's location enabling you to virtually walk through the property at your own speed. Virtual commerce combines the interactive visit explained above and the ability to make custom adjustments to the home. It works just like e-commerce. This is totally amazing since you get to play with designs. To use VR, you do not need complicated computers and materials like motion sensors. VR technology has made giant steps in the past year and its future is expected to be mobile, through apps. If your real estate agency has a mobile app then integrating VR is super easy. VR technology is a great opportunity for people in real estate. It does not cost an arm and a leg; it is easily incorporated in existing platforms. It is a perfect way to improve your sales efficiency with no need for additional staff. Virtual Reality technology is a gold mine. Giant corporations like Apple and Google are committing a lot of resources to it. Facebook bought Oculus Rift, a Virtual Reality star and even built a research lab named Area 404 to partially work on Virtual Reality. Steve Cuffari, a top CouponBox.com content marketing manager, said that investing into VR is a wise decision. He added that VR is no longer for gamers alone. It is now possible to virtually house shop, go on vacations or attend concerts and classes. How can you take advantage of this amazing technology and use it to earn money? The mere thought of creating a video game for VR using your own code may sound overwhelming. However, some corporations such as Steam are making it simple. Stephen R. Foster, a game creator, and Multi-Dimensional Games CEO, said that Steam allows you to build your own VR game and earn from it. He added that their secret is allowing developers to utilize HTML, JavaScript, and CSS (the Big Three front-end technologies). Their aim is making the creation of VR content almost as easy as creating a website. Who said that you must be a tech expert to earn revenue off VR? All you need to do is read a lot of content about VR and start blogging. Talk about various VR experiences, platforms, and apps. As your blog grows, you can earn from sponsorships and Google ad revenue. If you have a band that is 'not there' yet consider VR, it might help. VR technology can create virtual front-row concert seats from anywhere. Kore Asian Media, a Los Angeles based company, is banking on this. They are aiming at a world in which sold-out concerts will have unlimited –front-row seat tickets. For graphic designers, it is possible to get hired by a boutique VR corporation to build real estate in their games. A Talented VR designer can come up with a unique architecture style, virtually build it and maybe sell the templates to VR content creators. Real estate agents now have the luxury of showing houses without physical showings. Buyers can see as many houses as they want while saving time. A company like Walkthrough creates VR tours for agents to show listed properties to potential buyers. This technology also makes it possible to virtually test drive a boat or a car. Imagine teaching a university or college in another country from the comfort of your home. With VR an independent teacher or tutor can create an informative course and teach it anywhere.

Design, engineering, and other technical courses can now be taught digitally. VR is one of the best things that ever happened to the world. And being able to earn from it is even better. Almost all these methods do not even require you to leave your home. Pick the one that suits you and start earning. The VR era is just around the corner. When you see tech giants like Facebook, Google, Apple, and Microsoft investing billions in VR, then you know it's big, and it will get even bigger. Tech experts have confirmed that the VR revolution will surpass the mobile phone advent. The first company to build a VR product that appeals to the masses will achieve great victory—in a huge way. How is this important to designers? The market that has been their lifeline is almost changing to a new model. Touch, depth, emotion, and sound will all be incorporated into the VR experience, taking 2D screens off the market. You can only learn about virtual reality design in virtual reality. You cannot just be an observer. You must participate and even be able to affect the outcome. So, you first need to experience VR and understand its mechanics. You can start with Google Cardboard if you are a newbie. It is not expensive, and it is compatible with any smartphone. If you want the best experience and you can afford it then HTC Vive and Oculus Rift are perfect for you—you can interact with the virtual environment, and they come with natural hand controllers. For apps, Google Earth VR and Tilt Brush will do. Designing for rectangles is so natural since most viewing devices are rectangular. However, in 3600 spaces your environment is limitless. Think about what you want to create. Is it an educational app or an interactive movie? Designing a VR experience is more like creating a mobile product or website. It requires conceptual flows, personas, interaction models, and wireframes. As you memorize your design ideas, keep in mind the following. How or where do people start? What guides them without crushing them? Don't just expect users to know where to go and what to do automatically. Design your software for the user. Make the familiarization slow and progressive and include visual clues and guidance. Intuitive User Interfaces will make VR appealing to the masses. Consider the patterns that we have grown accustomed to like pinching to zoom, long tapping and swiping. VR should provide for them as well. New ones may come along, but for now, these could do. Put your ideas on paper. It is cheap and fast, and it is easier done on paper than with software. You could start with the tools you are familiar with like Sketch or use the opportunity to learn new ones. The engine you will use determines this. For 3D games, Unreal Engine or Unity is excellent. Also, for more elaborate creations use Maya and Cinema 4D. The three top frameworks for VR designs include. Daydream VR for mid-range VR. It is only compatible with mobile phones. Unreal SDK/Unity VR for high-end headsets like HTC Vive, Hololens (AR) and Oculus Rift. Mozilla A-frame for web VR - It is compatible with Samsung Gear, Google Cardboard and Oculus Rift. You need to understand your users and whatever may affect them as they experience VR. Sometimes, prolonged use of VR headset could cause nausea or fatigue. VR is confusing to the brain since your environment is moving, but your body is stationary. If your app has a lot of movement like jumping and accelerating, then your users must control it, or it will make them sick. Even in VR, there are issues like agoraphobia, vertigo, and claustrophobia. Understand and consider scale when designing for VR. Don't create a tiny space because users may get claustrophobic and in a huge one, they may get lost. Use non-spatial methods like light and audio to guide your users. Before designing for VR, learn and understand all the necessary comfortable range of motion zones. Poor posture can cause irreversible damage to a user's neck and spine. Let interaction with your VR device be as intuitive and as natural as possible. In VR you can't see your hands. Therefore, you must create hand controllers fit for blind mode use. The sound is a crucial part of VR since it does not have tactile feedback. When users touch things, sound could be used to give feedback. Designing for VR is very exciting, and your design could make headlines. This is an excellent opportunity to explore your full potential in designing. Augmented reality technology lays digital information and images over a real-life environment when they are viewed on a mobile device. It may sound new to you, but the technology has been there for over half a century. Morton Heilig, a cinematographer, invented the 3-D machine in 1962 which combined film with sensory stimuli creating an immersive environment. In the '90s Tom Caudell, a researcher, came up with the name "augmented reality" to refer to the graphical overlays that were used by technicians in the Boeing aircraft. The technology was refined to be used on smart devices in 2016 and advertiser interest to reach mobile consumers keeps growing. The interest to reach consumers digitally proves augmented reality useful in interaction and attraction of customers. Augmented reality incorporates 3-D digital images into real world locations. Companies that specialize in digital marketing maintain that businesses will be more interested in adding promotions and advertisements in public spaces during events. A few more examples of AR promotional images are life-sized virtual furniture, cars, and electronics. Companies can reach customers by using AR to enable them to view products more closely without going to the store. IKEA, a furniture retailer, released an app in addition to its print catalog. As a buyer browses the catalog, they can look at 3-D photos of the furniture. Virtual images are also available to allow them to see whether an individual piece can fit in their space. With AR some online stores don't even need to have a physical retail space. Shoppers can just have a look at the store's virtual image and even make their orders by tapping their phone screens. Search engine results combined with maps may help someone find products in their local area. However, most people cannot read maps correctly. Augmented reality apps are replacing the use of maps by allowing people to find what they need by imagery of their environment in real time. Companies are always competing for advertising space. AR eliminates this problem because companies can show virtual banners in a real-time environment. Graphically overlaying the location of a business offering discounts and coupons might grab a potential buyer's attention. Augmented Reality has been in existence for a very long time, only now it is more advanced. With the improvements, anyone can make money from it with a small amount of capital. With the fantastic and convenient methods of advertising, you don't need to compete for billboard space anymore. People have been waiting for VR to take off for years and they have been met with disappointment—until recently. A lot of evidence is now promising a bright future for VR, but investors should be knowledgeable about several things before diving in; like what the risks are, how big the market is going to be, why this strategy should be played out in the long term and who the key players are. Here is what you should know before investing in VR. According to Grand View Research estimates, the global VR market might be worth $48.5 billion by 2025. That is just the top-end estimation, other estimates range from $7.5-22.5 billion. A year ago, the VR market was worth only $1.8 billion, which implies that VR is destined to grow largely. Anyone looking to invest in VR should know that the technology is likely to take more time before it takes off, especially because virtual reality hardware is very expensive. Remember when Facebook's (NASDAQ: FB) Oculus launched the high-end Rift headset. The device was priced at $599 and its Touch controllers at $199. That was too costly for most consumers and Oculus had to reduce the price of the VR package twice. It is now priced at $399 for both the controllers and headsets. But still, not many people have an extra $400 to buy VR equipment so for a while, these prices will bar many potential consumers from high-end VR tech. Moreover, this high-end equipment needs a lot of processing power to provide high quality graphics with low latency (for the virtual environment to move smoothly as the user moves). There are many investment avenues in VR for an investor to choose from. For example, an investor interested in chipmakers can invest in NVIDIA, which makes GPUs (Graphics Processing Units). 53% of NVIDIA's revenue is generated by the gaming segment which makes the corporation a key player in the VR space. There is also Alphabet's (NASDAQ: GOOG) (NASDAQ: GOOGL) Google, for anyone looking for solid software and hardware. NVIDIA, Facebook, and Google are not the only players in VR. There are other companies that are looking to venture into VR for more growth. Sony (NYSE: SNE) acquired an advantage in the console market when it launched its PlayStation VR headsets that are compatible with the current versions of PlayStation 4. Intel (NASDAQ: INTC) has also made moves expressing their interest in VR. Many companies involving themselves in VR are also getting involved in AR. Augmented reality is so much entwined into VR and both might be of great benefit to investors. Google has invested greatly in VR, but it also re-launched the Google Glass device. According to Mark Zuckerberg, CEO of Facebook, it might take VR five to ten years to completely take off. If a tech billionaire is investing for the long haul, then you should consider playing the long game with VR investments as well. All the companies above are not betting entirely on VR and they are not earning any significant profit from it now. But they have all created a long-term strategy to benefit later. Investors should copy that approach. Blockchain is the fundamental technology that supports the bitcoin network, and it has acquired extensive adoption across numerous industries. VIBEHub seems to be pushing these limits even further by incorporating blockchain technology into Virtual Reality to come up with the first ever Virtual Reality decentralized marketplace in the world. Augmented Reality and Virtual reality have gained a lot of interest over the recent years because of their capacity to basically change the user experience on practically any platform that requires customer interaction. Nowadays, visual technology is being utilized in e-commerce, entertainment, education, medicine, and many other segments. VIBEHub aims at offering an unlimited virtual universe by integrating cryptocurrency technology into Artificial Reality/Virtual Reality technology. By doing so, this corporation is forming the foundation to start a technology revolution with an estimated value of $162 billion by 2020. VIBEHub users will be allowed to buy and sell experiences that cannot be accomplished with traditional technology: a virtual meet-and-greet with your best artist who lives across the world, a virtual front seat at a live concert, guitar, boxing, yoga lessons with a life-sized instructor sitting in front of the user. The opportunities for monetizing this platform for users are astronomical and countless. Tutors and artists will be able to reach thousands or even millions of fans in a single stream and charge a premium price for streams in Augmented Reality—something they cannot do at the moment. VIBEHub has entered the scene at a very good time when high-value VR devices can be purchased anywhere for $70-$400. The influence of blockchain technology and the VIBE token can monetize this new virtual world. VIBEHub is in beta testing; that is the most impressive thing about them. They already launched a beta channel of their own on the world-famous Oculus platform which anyone can try out today. Their Virtual reality work is of high quality, ranked among the best globally. VIBEHub's Virtual Reality development uses SteamVR SDK, Unity Engine, Microsoft HoloLens SDK, Sony PSVR SDK and Oculus SDK. This combination of technologies will facilitate a cross-platform product that works with both existing and future hardware. With this kind of cross-compatibility, VIBEHub is expected to become a universal marketplace for all high-tech visual needs. The body tracking of avatars and voice chat in the virtual environment will use P2P technologies allowing massive user scaling while containing costs at the same time. After the token sale VIBEHub will incorporate the use of unique multi-sensor stereographic cameras to achieve "HoloPresence". "HoloPresence" is a technology demonstrated by the research team at Microsoft in the "HoloPortation" project. According to VIBEHub, this is the actual future in Virtual Reality technology. This is the first decentralized marketplace of its kind, and it is much anticipated. The VIBEHub official token sale began on August 22nd, for more information on VIBEHub visit vibehub.io.

Chapter 6
Buy Real Estate in the Metaverse

Did you know that you can earn as much as 5,000 dollars just from buying property in the metaverse? Well, ever since people realized that you could earn some good money in metaverse by buying land, the number of metaverse users suddenly increased. Imagine being able to earn $6,000 from renting a room that is 16 by 16 meters square. But how can you buy land from metaverse? Decentraland is one of the largest and most popular platforms that users can purchase land from. Currently, the number of their users has superseded 20 million. It has also hosted the largest concert of all time. In simple terms, it is a virtual space where users can meet for social interactions such as playing video games, visiting sites, and going to the movies. With this platform, you can do anything you think of. Now the big question is, how can you buy property in the metaverse from Decentraland? Steps to Follow When Buying Property in Metaverse - I). First things first, you must identify the property that has caught your eye. Check out the price, size, and location of the property. It is as simple as buying property in the physical world. II). Now that you have identified the property, let's say the property is worth 3890 mana. Mana is the currency that is used in the metaverse virtual world and the least land you can buy is worth 3890 mana. Every metaverse virtual world has its currency. Therefore, if you want to purchase any property from their metaverse, you will need to have their currency. III). As we have seen earlier, it will cost 3890 Mana for you to purchase land from Decentraland. Currently, one-man costs $2.70. This number is expected to rise as metaverse popularity increases. How can Decentraland Earn you Money? There are many ways you can make money from this virtual land. One of the ways is through buying and selling NFTs in the form of music, art, and digital apparel called Wearables. This virtual land is divided into 90256 square meter parcels where each parcel has its own verified NFT. This means that it is unique, and you cannot forget it. Upland is the second most popular platform that you can buy virtual land from. The developers of this technology are trying to replicate it to make it look like the real world. In this case, they take the features of some popular cities in the United States and transfer them to virtual land. That way, if you want to buy property in let's say, New York or San Francisco, you can just do it by going to Upland and purchasing it. Another amazing feature of this platform is that it works like a Google map. Where you can zoom the property, you want or a post that has been erected on the street and buy it if you want. What Upland is trying to achieve is the complete replica of their platform to the real world.

Also, they give bonuses to people who sign up for their technology, gamify their games to make them more interesting and appealing to the buyers, and in turn, they earn their owners more money. Cryptovoxels is a unique platform that allows the users not only to buy land but also to build on it as well as display their NFTs. One of the main advantages of Cryptovoxels is that it is cheaper compared to other platforms. From as low as 1.46 ETH, you can get a nice piece of land. Currently, Somnium Space version of the metaverse is still in development. But from the look of things, it's going to be super cool. You will be able to zoom any property that has caught your eye and buy it if you want. For instance, if you want to visit Singapore to buy land in the virtual world. All you must do is go in and find what pleases you in Singapore, zoom and look at its features then buy it. The graphics and features of this version will blow your mind when the project is completed. Right now, all we can do is wait and see what they have in store for us. The world's first Real estate metaverse company was developed by Metaverse Properties. If we compare Decentraland and Metaverse Property, both versions have similar features, but the latter has the most profound properties that make it unique. It has the most momentum, volume and not to mention you can make money through this version of the metaverse compared to the others. What makes Metaverse Properties stand out is that they use REIT which stands for (real estate investment trust) to invest money in real estate. They later give the money back to the shareholders based on the income they have generated. It's safe to say that this project will be of great success when the company gets the project up and running. How are the Platforms Comparable in Terms of Buying Property? Currently, you need to have $10,000 to purchase a piece of land in Decentraland. If you decide to go with Cryptovoxels metaverse, you will require $5,000. But if you decide to forgo the prices of buying the property in these two versions and decide to look at what you stand to gain later, With Decentraland you will not be disappointed. Finally, there are many metaverses in the world you can buy virtual property from. It can be a little bit confusing to the users especially if you have just joined metaverse. The five versions that we have discussed are at the top of our list. They will assist you to better understand how buying property in the virtual land works and if you still have some trouble getting around metaverse, you can do thorough research from the internet. You can also buy real estate in the real world using the Algorand blockchain. The company associated with Algorand is Lofty AI. Algorand blockchain has some of the lowest fees and the tokens from Lofty AI will be stored in your Algo wallet. Tokens represent a fraction of ownership in real estate all over the United States and eventually around the world.

Chapter 7
NFT and Crypto

An NFT (non-fungible token) is a unique and non-interchangeable unit of data stored on a blockchain like Algorand or Ethereum, a form of digital ledger for recording transactions. NFTs can be associated with digital files such as photos, videos, and audio and now gaming. Metaverse is a virtual world that allows users to be linked to virtual reality just like the World Wide Web. If you are not an outdoorsy person, metaverse has got you covered. Imagine being able to attend office meetings, go to concerts, gaming, learn, go on dates without leaving your apartment. With this new technology, everything you think of will be possible. But how will this work? How Metaverse Works in The Virtual World - Are you familiar with the game PUBG? Now, this game allows players as many as four to join the same group and later play. During the game, you can also engage in other activities while at it. Now comes a metaverse that will allow users to enter the PUBG GROUND. Players will be able to talk, walk, shop, while still playing. Pretty cool, right! This is what technology is all about; allowing users to experience a new level of fun. If you have some trouble understanding the idea, ENDER'S GAME, which is a Hollywood movie, will certainly explain the concept of metaverse further. Assuming you are in a different state like Seattle, and you want to attend a meeting that is in New York as well as save a couple of bucks". In the metaverse, you will be able to attend the meetings, chat with your colleagues, and even talk to your boss without meeting in person. By 2030, the virtual world would have taken over the globe. Currently, some of the big tech companies are working to ensure they are not left behind when this move takes its course. Google began working on the project a few years back and now, Facebook along with Microsoft have jumped right into the idea. One of the main goals of Crypto is to decentralize the technology. They want to achieve this by ensuring users have control of their items, let's say currency. Metaverse is also based on this concept. As we all know, Cryptocurrencies work entirely on decentralized systems. There are no third parties. Users can exchange items one on one. When we compare the two technologies, we can all see that they are closely related. Unfortunately, Crypto and NFT cannot be operated in an imaginative world. 2021 has brought a lot of changes. We can socialize and interact with each other through the internet. Metaverse has created a platform where all this is possible. These two technologies are comparable in some respects. NFT through metaverse allows its users to take control of the ownership of some of their assets. You are allowed to have full access to videos, pictures, and not to mention real estate. Also, through NFT, you can purchase, sell, and transfer items within metaverse or the internet. Now, it is easier to perform all these activities without worrying about how the transactions will be made as the world is embracing digital artwork. Does NFT and its Relation to Metaverse Still Confuse you? It is no doubt that NFT and metaverse will have a huge impact on the world of technology. And as we have seen earlier, players can purchase, sell pictures and music videos on NFT platforms. The pictures might be of no use to you currently. After all, what will a virtual picture help you with anyway? but with the metaverse, everything changes. You will be allowed to use everything you bought on their platform as you please. It is believed that NFT will be the face of the metaverse and that everything you buy from the virtual world will be sold and bought by the NFT technology. We can still have a look at the same example that we had earlier. If you want to attend a meeting that is in a different state. You will probably require a couple of things for the meeting. You might want a suit or rather some nice office wear shoes. This is where NFT comes in, you can purchase all these items through their platform and use them in your virtual meeting. When you want to meet your girlfriend for dinner and require a bouquet, NFT provides you the platform to buy them. In addition, you will have to purchase the virtual land from metaverse through NFT marketplaces to enjoy the full experience metaverse offers. From what we can see, it is safe to conclude that the two technologies are related. How Will Metaverse and NFT Influence the Growth of the Market? When we went from watching 3D pictures, 5D sounds, playing virtual video games, we all thought that that was probably it. But with the combination of the two technologies, we expect our minds to be blown away. The outcome is expected to be far much better than what we already have seen and experienced. Currently, these Big Tech companies are developing products that can be used in the virtual world. Companies like Facebook, Google, and Microsoft envision a world where virtual reality will take over the world. They are looking forward to a future where everything is possible through virtual reality. Where users from different parts of the world can meet, have coffee, and even explore the world together. After October 2021 when the CEO of Facebook announced that his company is formalizing the future of his company on metaverse, several NFT and CRYPO companies rushed to add metaverse on their servers. How will Facebook's Metaverse Support NFT? Mark Zuckerberg announced during the conference that his company will allow the usage of NFTs into the blockchain platforms since they have grown in masses over the years. The Head of Facebook's Metaverse Product pointed out in the conference that they intended on allowing its users to make purchases of digital goods where they can be able to display them for reselling to other users. How Will Buying and Selling of NFTs in the Metaverse Work? With the advancement of the metaverse, tech companies are working to ensure they are not left behind. This brings us to this question: who stands to benefit more when this technology reaches its maturity? Companies that would have created copies of their products in line with the virtual world and ready their teams for the move will stand to benefit the most. This will also include virtual consumers that would have understood how this technology works. In conclusion, the entire concept of a metaverse world is still in its infancy stage. It is only after the completion of this technology that users will be able to exhaust their full potential. NFT along with the metaverse wants a universe where everything imaginative will be experienced like the real world. Are you looking towards making extra cash from NFTs? If you are, you've come to the right place where tech gurus and firms have discovered new uses for cryptocurrencies and other technological advancements that will transform the digital world. This chapter is going to provide you with a clear guideline on how to sell your NFTs. Before you sell your NFT. It must have a digital certificate to show ownership. Normally, this certificate is created on the blockchain network called Ethereum or minted on a blockchain like Algorand. You can create any digital content to be an NFT like a picture, a video game or music bearing in mind the money you make will depend on your creativity, your reputation, and the quality. In every business that people venture into, the first thing they look for is the market. Is the market-friendly? Am I going to earn profits? are some of the questions they ask. So, look at it as Amazon or NFT but items are sold in a digital form. There are several marketplaces where you can sell your NFT. And several of them specialize in unique digital assets. Currently, OpenSea hosts the largest marketplace. It provides a large market of NFTs. After you have selected the market, use a cryptocurrency wallet, and select the option "Mint your NFT" then upload your file. Each marketplace has its process of minting the NFT from one click to several clicks. It is also important to note that monetizing your work with royalties is done during the minting process. When the minting process is complete you will be presented with an option that states "list your NFT" Click on the option and follow the steps that will be provided. These steps will have details like the price, auction time, and type of cryptocurrency that you accept. If you want to sell or transfer your NFT to other marketplaces you should be aware of the additional fee that you will incur for the process. A transaction fee will be calculated. This fee is normally the Ethereum network's fee which serves the purposes of handling the transaction. Note that this fee varies depending on the number of users of the network at that time. Also, each marketplace has a fee that is charged for the sale. This fee is deducted from the percentage of the final sale price of the NFT. After the listing process, your NFT is now ready for sale. The final and the most important step is promoting the NFT. If you want to make a quick sale you must be creative, promoting the NFT on your social media and website will lead to a quick sale. Bear in mind any changes you make to the listing will incur additional charges that will affect your profit in the long run. Anyone can sell their NFTs and not only digital creators. If for instance, you bought your NFT from a collector or a creator, you can list the NFT for sale. How Can You Sell an NFT You Just Bought? When you want to sell an NFT that you purchased, you will still be required to follow the same process of listing an NFT except "Minting the NFT". From there, move it to the marketplace to make it available. If it's already transferred, you don't need to repeat the process once again. Click on the button to sell and there you have it! Your NFT is ready for purchase. Note that the handling fee and royalty charges set by the creator will still apply. When is the Right Time to Sell NFT? It is not an easy task selling an NFT especially if you want to sell it at a higher price than you bought. Selling it depends on what you are selling, why you are selling, and who you are selling it to. If you are a content creator, minting and selling NFTs can be a good way for you to earn some extra "bucks". Keep tabs on the interest of the NFT to ensure that you can sell it when the prices are higher. Also, you need to keep in mind the handling fee that affects your profit when you make changes on the NFT. For instance, if the Ethereum network fee increases, this will automatically lower the profit of your sale. If you want to sell your NFT on the basis that it has depreciated, you are not interested in it anymore, or you want to invest the money somewhere else, then you can sell it. Before you get all excited, first you need to calculate your possible profit or loss after deducting the handling fee and the royalty charges imposed by the creator. You can avoid higher charges of the Ethereum network by timing when the network is not congested. Selling an NFT is not a walk in the park, there's a lot of work to be done to make it possible. From ensuring good timing in the Ethereum network to avoid congestion to marketing it on the social media networks. If you are a content creator looking for a business to venture into, NFT can be a good investment for you. It will offer you a new platform to explore your skills. Algorand blockchain has the lowest fees and offer great security when it comes to NFTS. At some point in life, we have all heard or come across identify theft where a person's name and personal information are stolen. Even in the virtual world identity theft can happen. The creation of highly sophisticated games that have multiplayer and the technological advancement surrounding the metaverse might bring a challenge to security. These advancements require a lot of time and money to ensure they are secure. So, how can we ensure that the metaverses are safe and secure? For one, the metaverses developers need to come up with better ways that are advanced and that can match the technology that is currently being used in the metaverse. They can decide to generate unique codes that will be impossible to replicate. So that, if you need let's say create some content, no one can claim ownership or rather use them without the codes. Look at it like the genetic codes that are used to confirm the identity of a person. NFTs can provide the solution to the problem of insecurity. The sale of memes, digital art, and playing cards has been so huge in the last few years that it has taken the world by surprise. Shockingly, this year's sale of US $69.3 million seems to be the tip of the iceberg from what NFT offers in general. If digital concert tickets can be stored in the blockchain to protect the rights and ownership of their creator or the user, why not virtual identity? There are always loopholes in every technology. With that said, 100% guarantee that technology can have unbreakable security is next to impossible. But with blockchain effectiveness and its decentralization, assures users a new level of experience that will make it easier to protect their identity for them to move freely in the metaverse. The COO of Crypto.com Eric Anziani said that NFT would enable its users to showcase their skills and have an identity across their platforms. This identity will assist the users to have ownership of their content and therefore, selling and trading of their items would be made easier. He later pointed out that several digital platforms were open to the idea of users having identity across platforms and some companies had started using it. It is not an easy task to provide digital or rather virtual reality players security that is impenetrable by other networks. A lot of time and money must be spent to make this possible. NFT offers its users the freedom to choose and develop what interests them based on the social, economic, and political life of the world. NFT databases can offer a more secure identity in virtual reality than you can get in the real world. Passwords can be stolen, passports duplicated, and biometrics can be hacked. With NFT, blockchain can secure your identity and ensure nothing is replicated. The idea of allowing identity in the metaverse is to enable people to move freely in the metaverse and to create a platform where users can explore and exhaust these worlds. The breakthrough of NFT may be found from the origins of adopting human movement from the physical to the virtual world, as well as from one metaverse to the next while creating and securing a strong identity for the users. This was the point Anziani was trying to convey moving from a "closed-loop" to an "open-loop". His message also emphasized the amazing opportunities NFT would continue to offer even in the future. He added that currently, trading assets is what was trending in the metaverse and that there was still a lot to be discovered and developed. Amazingly, users want a stable and secure platform. Yet NFTs open some possibilities of a disabled identity that in turn provides great opportunities for fun. To what extent is the fun? Can the identities be rented? Can we trade aspects of our identity? Can we mint multiple identities? I am positive those are the questions running into your mind. With NFT, all these scenarios are possible. NFT: How is NFT Promoting Growth in the

Metaverse Community? We have already established that there are great opportunities in the metaverse. Currently, NFT is inspiring communities around the metaverse. Communities that come together to generate projects like PFP avatar and strange text files. These communities have grown in numbers to even reach tens of thousands of users with other members who are collectors trading or selling their items. A scheme by the name Loot Project that converts gaming material or rather treasures such as "short swords" and "divine slippers" into collectible and later ranked by rarity, traded a collectible for US $800,000. According to Anziani, such communities are strong, and they are transforming small opportunities into large profit-making businesses. He also added that such communities were important now that social networking platforms were investing in the metaverse, and they intended on transforming the "open-loop philosophy" to a "closed-loop philosophy". Also, he explained that User-created metaverses enabled by NFT would be the beginning of a new era of freedom in cyberspace. He went ahead to note that NFT would open a kind of social network web 3.0 that would give the user more freedom and less centralized oversight. His conclusion was, eventually people would shift their focus that was in the "close-loop" and go for the "open-loop" metaverses which were logical and allowed its players to use their identities however they liked in different environments and for various activities all through NFT. Imagine a virtual world where you will be able to visit sites, go shopping, drive across town, and meet at a café with friends. All these scenarios will be made possible in the virtual world. You will be able to accomplish all your imaginations thanks to the rapid advancement of this technology. Metaverse is not a new technology. It has been there for some time. The only difference is that decades ago, the new advancements that we are seeing now had not been developed. They existed in the form of multiple online playing games. Currently, we are on another level that brings out the true meaning of fun and opportunities, and sooner, we will enter an era that will not be distinguishable from the real world.

Companies Like Decentraland and Somnium Space have already begun to develop their new societies. With the users trading items, settling the land, and interacting through games. For a society to function, it needs a stable and working economy. Every digital item is verified in the metaverse from cars, clothing, pictures, and buildings. This in turn ensures that the economy is secure and functioning. For the metaverse to grow, it will need the freedom to move to other metaverses trading, selling, and even purchasing. Digital assets are stored in the blockchain. With NFT, the authentication process will be smooth. Every item will be verified, and this will ensure that identity theft is not achievable. NFTs are protected by a key called a cryptographic key. This key ensures users' data and personal information is not hacked or even replicated. Also, it guarantees there is a strong verification process to protect the user's possessions. Apart from NFTs selling their arts at large sums of money, they also open new opportunities where users can engage freely, sign contracts, have independent ownership of property just like the real world. The COO of Crypto.com Eric Anziani pointed out that aside from NFT being recognized for digital art, it was going to be the platform that will represent any item or asset in the metaverses in the future. The Metaverse: How is Property Developed in the Metaverse? When you log in to Decentraland, there are so many activities that you will find. You will meet people chatting by the fountains, guests walking in a casino, and people going to movie theaters. All these activities are achievable with the aid of virtual world real estate development. People buy land and build scenarios that happen in real life but the metaverse. This technology has not reached its completion and there is still a lot to be done to make the physical and the virtual world similar. Some of these creators say that the technology is still in its early stages. But this has not stopped people from flocking the metaverse in search of new business opportunities, social interactions, as well as exploring the metaverse. Note that, the value of the virtual land will depend on the place you want to purchase that land. For instance, if you want a place that resembles Beverly Hills, it will come at a high cost. The notion of Decentraland and other metaverse economic development relies on their closeness of land. All metaverses border each other and on a specific location. This concept in turn results in a shortage of goods and services. Scarcity raises the prices of items and property based on the law of demand and supply. Property possession, selling, and trading of items in the metaverse are all handled by NFT. It provides proof of ownership of land, a building, or and any other item. Anziani pointed out that, NFT database was impossible to replicate or corrupt due to the smart system that has been put in place to prevent any duplication. He further explained that if you owned property or an asset in the metaverse and you have all the documents and files for proof, you can claim the ownership rights of that property. Is Property in the Metaverse Worth all the Hype? Currently, real estate is a booming business in the metaverse. These came after the evolution and advancement of the real estate industry. In June, a parcel of land in Decentraland sold for $900,000; it was purchased by Republic Realm, a company that specializes in digital investment. This company is aiming at transforming the digital land into a mall that will be called Metajuku named after Harajuku which is a district in Tokyo. These are the activities that will bring investment opportunities to the metaverse, Real estate investment funds (REITs) have begun their plans to shift their businesses in it. Corroborating what the creators had hoped for when they launched it in 2017. A proposal by Decentraland to its application developers was that they take full sponsorship of the economic interactions between the users and their applications. One of the metaverse declarations reads that "for the economic interaction to work, three things have to be traded: currency, goods, and services". When metaverse was first developed the fashion industry was the first to join in. And over the years this industry has seen tremendous growth. Louis Vuitton developed its own video game called LOUIS THE GAME and another company like Luxury house Burberry created accessories that were used to play a video game in the Blankos

Block Party. A shoemaker of metaverse sneakers has recently posted over millions of dollars in sales. He designs unique sneakers and sells them through NFT for players. More people are open to the idea of Cryptos. Five months ago, there were 100 million users. Currently, the number of users is at 200 million and this number is expected to go up". says Anziani. He strongly believes that the combination of virtual worlds and blockchain will result in the tremendous growth of metaverse.

Chapter 8

Make Money in the Metaverse

As mentioned earlier, technology is revolving around the metaverse, and companies are in a rush to make sure they are not left behind. Now that we know about metaverse and what it entails, the big question remains, how can users make money through it? We are going to look at eleven ways and let you decide which is the best way for you. Currently, NFT art is what is new and trending! And if you look it up, you will see that recently there are multiple news articles about a piece of NFT art that had hit a new record price. A couple of years ago, someone bought a Bored Ape NFT for $50 and later sold it at 1.8 million dollars. Amazing, right? So, you can buy NFT art and put it on the metaverse and later sell the art at a higher price. Remember the idea is to earn some extra cash. Voxels are this cool material that is used to build items on the metaverse. For instance, they can be used to construct buildings, clothes, cars, and other items. If you are a gaming guru, then you are familiar with the game Minecraft. This game brings a clear picture of what voxels are. You can decide to buy these voxels and sell them to the players. This is a lucrative business in the metaverse world. Since the constant evolution of the metaverse, there are many activities that you can do now as opposed to when it was first introduced. one being construction. Yes, I mean construction! One of the amazing features that have been introduced in the metaverse is construction. There are some construction companies on it. How does it work? If you want a building to be constructed, you must pass by the right channels. Look for a company that will take it from the ground up. Meaning, you must have an architect. Some of these companies are making as high as $300,000 per project. A company like

Voxel Architects makes this amount for one project. For some reason, Real Estate companies have been increasing daily. Companies like Sandbox and Decentraland have been making millions from real estate. If you can start a real estate company that will list plots of land for sale, you can get some good cash out of it! The idea of metaverse was to bring every imaginative concept into reality. And just like the real world, you can advertise your items on metaverse. You can erect a post on the street or rather build advertising signage on your building. A company like Nike is trying to catch up with this new technology by developing a platform on the metaverse where they can do their advertisement from. I am sure you have come across a sign or a post that says, "there's a piece of land that you can rent and for more information call the number below". Just like the real world, you can rent your building or office space to other metaverse users called Parcel Rentals. If you are not sure of what you will do with the land you have bought, renting that piece of land might be a pretty good idea. Gaming is an industry that has been booming for some years now. It is an industry that is growing constantly. New games are being developed that are more advanced and interesting than the previous games. And with this growth comes great offers. Platforms are being developed like MMORPGs which have their currencies and land. Also, you can build your games from platforms like Sandbox and Decentraland. If you develop interesting games and casinos, you stand a chance of making good money once more virtual reality is introduced. Imagine a virtual universe where games like bowling alleys, laser tag arenas, and even ax throwing are introduced. How cool will that universe be? This might sound silly, but Karaoke is the next real big thing in the metaverse. Although it might be difficult to get together with your friends at the same time, once you do, you will be in for some treats. The question is, how can you make money with karaoke? Well, start with a karaoke bar or rather create your own NFT music and sell it to other karaoke bars. Also, hosting speed dating and trivia nights can be your ticket to earning money. You do not have to worry anymore about where you can get your avatar clothes from. These virtual worlds got you covered. Currently, some designers have built their business around making avatar clothes. Surprisingly, there is a company that has bought $2million inland within Decentaland fashion industry just to sell virtual clothing. Although you cannot transfer your virtual clothing from one metaverse to another, you can resale the clothes at a higher price. Adding collectibles to your list is not a bad idea. Just like in the real world you can collect your valuables and trade them. Collectables like clothes, cars, and jewelry, can fill your pockets. These collectibles are NFTs meaning they have unique features that cannot be duplicated. From Voxels, you can make collectibles and later sell them on metaverse markets. If you are a data and analytics person, I am sure you are wondering how much data metaverses are gathering. Just like the searches we do in the real world and the internet records the data, metaverses also collect data from the searches and the places we visit frequently. From the data that is collected, store owners can get a glimpse of how frequent their stores have been visited, a real estate agent can see how many people have clicked on his advertisement, and an NFT music seller can see how much of his music has been sold. In conclusion, metaverse has created great opportunities for people to make money. There are several ways for you to do so, but you must think outside the box. And since metaverse technology keeps on advancing, there will be a lot you can do in the years to come. Drone Racing will also implement ways to make money called play to earn on the Algorand blockchain. This will ensure more companies introduce this style of play on blockchains to bring more users from the gaming world.

Conclusion

Seemingly, blockchain will take over most aspects governing the world of finance, and probably become the milestone to advance in financial institutions and other aspects of the industry. The first and most important thing about blockchain is the technical features enable transactions between anonymous people, while still making the system secure for everyone. Better yet, since the system is not subject to regulation by banks or governments, it offers an unprecedented leverage for users over most other financial services. Among the multitude of bodies looking into the efficiency of blockchain, banks have been on the frontline to understand the technology benefits in the cost advantages as well as its efficiency. One of the ways the technology seems helpful for banks is its distributed ledger, which makes it ideal for reducing profit loss incurred by banks to uphold infrastructure that supports transactions across borders. This aspect also has a major impact with compliance, regulation, and security on trading as well. This outcome has seen over 40 banks across the world join R3 CEV, which is a body working on the technology regarding distributed ledgers. And according to the consortium, the efforts are promising and could turn out to offer benefits to banks across the globe. Another potential benefit is shortening the time taken in settling trades. The current time taken in carrying out this process takes up to three days for corporate bonds, stocks, mutual fund shares, and municipal securities. But others like foreign exchange settlements usually take two days, while Treasury bonds require a day or so. However, the use of blockchain can solve the riddle of condensing the time, which has haunted financial institutions for years. Thanks to this tech, such risks as counterparty risks can also decrease. The other area where this technology will most likely be useful is the insurance sector. Since insurance firms need to maintain massive records for their customer premiums, payments, and claims, having the best technology for this purpose can be far-reaching. Besides, with the risk of fraud looming large, the necessity for a secure system of records is inevitable. The use of blockchain services in the public sector becomes more efficient through filling the loopholes in the systems. Information on such services as vehicle registry, citizen identity, tax payments, and pensions can be fed into blockchain for secure storage. The tech can also be ideal for industries dealing with gigantic quantities of information like the media, music, diamond, and healthcare among others, most of which are already embracing the use of the technology. There is much to be done with blockchain technology, all the way from financial institutions themselves to the other areas like government and regulation.

As much as the digital revolution has seen changes in the media, it has also affected the finance world, thanks to the fact that both sections rely on computers. However, although there have been several changes over the last few decades, the cross-border transactions are yet to be revolutionized so far. This has seen banks resort to using complicated infrastructure in efforts to send money across borders, some of which have been in place since the 1970s. But blockchain can change all this through the creation of direct links between banks and getting rid of correspondent banking altogether. Banks can thus keep track of transactions as well as settle and clear them without turning to a central database or any other centralized management system. This area involves more than just keeping track of the transactions. In 2016, Ethereum initiated a blockchain project that was meant to reflect the crowdfunding market whereby a percentage contribution determines the percentage vote on how the fund should be used. As such, private companies can sell and trade in shares with the use of blockchain technology. The policy in trading using paperwork comes down to clearing and settlement taking up to three days after finalizing a trade. Blockchain technology is out to change this for the better, since it allows for the entire process involving execution, clearing, as well as the settlement of the trade to be carried out at the trading stage. Besides, such aspects as digital ownership and cryptographic keys progresses instantaneously to reduce the risk of counterparty and latency after the trade. Thanks to the fact that blockchain can provide transparent and accessible yet safe system records, the technology is one of the best tools regulators can use. Perhaps the best thing about blockchain is that it can be coded to carry out the authorization that goes in line with regulatory reporting. Another area with potential for change is the use of digital property, which can be copied, rather than the former bits and bytes. This efficiency has seen digital code gain value, and bitcoin is one of the leaders in the creation of this technology. The good news is that it goes a long way to preventing double spending or creation of counterfeit, which can be a plus for financial institutions as well. Every technological revolution must go through several challenges over time, and blockchain has seen its fair share along the way. For some, the technology is given too much credit, but it has its limitations, and some even believe that blockchain are not as effective for digital interactions as they should be. However, with all the developments and mistakes encountered along the way, some of the current limitations and issues clouding the technology have become clear. The speed at which a chain can execute a transaction is crucial to its performance if there is a transaction fee imposed, and then it becomes a matter of concern. The usefulness of any blockchain also comes into play when you factor in that these chains can also be used politically to store information. This brings concern of over 'bloating", which has seen criticism since miners have to repeat processing and recording of the information. Blockchain can use large networks to keep attacks at bay. But the very aspect that makes the technology sturdy can turn out to be a complication that drags it down. If the network is not robust enough with a wide distribution of nodes, it can prove difficult to bear any benefit for the users. The question of whether this is a critical flaw or just a problem with permissioned blockchain is still subject to discussion. It is apparent that blockchain technology has embraced a new approach to vocabulary, with cryptography taking center stage. But one thing remains for sure; blockchain features a lot of jargon. However, there are efforts underway to create easier indexes and glossaries. Protocols can be used for governance models, and the fact that miners are working on yet another incentivized model for governance; there is every opportunity for criticism. The blockchain world has seen many of these contentions, especially on the aspect of 'forking' a blockchain, which involves updating the chain protocol with consent from most users. Just as it is the case with any other decentralized database, blockchain have little margin for error when it comes to feeding the information. Accuracy is crucial in these chains, and the possibility of human error leading to big problems can be overwhelming. Another possible and almost inevitable problem with blockchain is security flaws that will spread with about half the computers working as nodes. The phenomenon is known as '51% attack,' and it is one of the warnings pointed out by Satoshi Nakamoto during the launching of bitcoin. So, the community keeps a keen eye on blockchain mining pools.

About the Author

Adidas Wilson was born in Chicago, Illinois, surviving a near death experience driving off a bridge in an 18 wheeler and getting hit by a train. Adidas has dedicated his time and effort to educate, motivate, and inspire people around the world to make positive lifestyle changes. Adidas enrolled at the University of Phoenix graduating with a bachelor's in Healthcare Management. Also studying Health care Informatics - Master Degree program at Lipscomb University. Amazon Best Seller's List and mentioned in Entrepreneur Magazine.

www.ingramcontent.com/pod-product-compliance
Ingram Content Group UK Ltd.
Pitfield, Milton Keynes, MK11 3LW, UK
UKHW021655190726
13853UKWH00001B/271